Contents

Helpful Tips
& Tricks
....
4

No-Braid Hangings

Fuzzy
Creature
Hangings
....
5

Maxi-Sox
Creatures
....
9

Four-Strand Creatures

Buggy
Fours
....
10

Centipedes
....
12

Bat Cat &
Meow Pal
....
13

Six-Strand Zipper Pulls and Key Chains

Teeny
Legs
....
14

Pretzel
Ears
....
16

Glow
Ghosts
....
17

Beady
Eyes
....
17

Snake
Key Chain
....
18

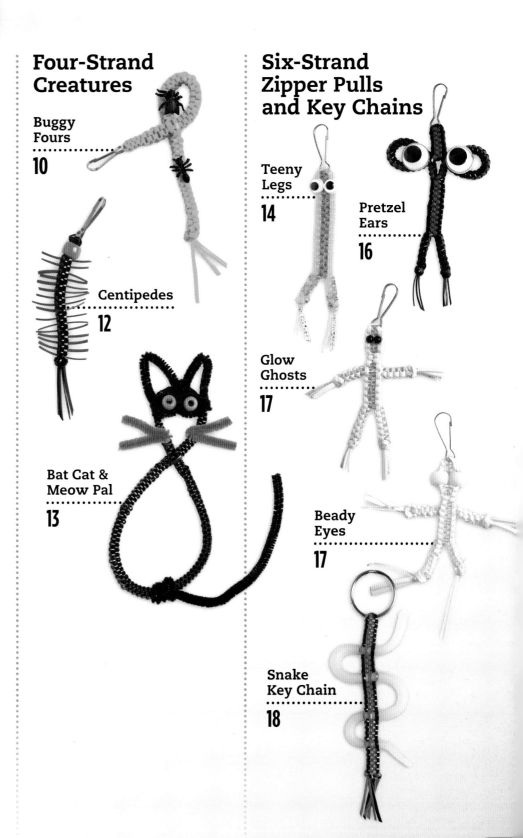

Helpful Tips & Tricks

Finding Materials: Most craft materials can be found in specialty craft stores and craft departments of variety stores and fabric stores. Animals and insects are sold in toy and educational stores, and many variety stores.

Variations and Substitutions: You can substitute materials for those suggested in this book. For example, witches' hats can be made of black felt, paper or foam, or they can be purchased as ready-made hats.

Plastic Canvas: The size of the plastic canvas used to make hangings can vary from that suggested under Materials. For instance, if you use a 1-inch pom-pom instead of a 2-inch pom-pom for the head, you would need less width and less length—say 6 by 20 instead of 8 by 26. Just leave enough room for your fingers to stitch up the last seam!

Lacing the Plastic Canvas: Either flat or round plastic lace can be used; be careful not to twist the flat lace as you weave.

Don't leave open spaces in front where the eyes and mouth will be glued. From the bottom hole, all laces should either emerge towards the front (outside) or towards the back (inside). You can skip one to three holes in front, but none in back.

Gluing: Gluing plastic to plastic requires a strong bonding agent. We recommend parental guidance when you come to this stage. Read the warning labels on the glue. Regular tacky glues work on the hair and other soft materials like paper and felt.

Flipping: Below we show the variations possible in one basic hanging (**a**) by (**b**) flipping it and (**c**) adding acrylic hair.

Hanging: To hang your creatures, use plastic lace, thread, or string. Cut a piece, and attach each end to the top row of plastic canvas on the right and on the left.

Fuzzy Creature Hangings

These easy to make decorations can be as wacky or scary as you like and require no complex knotting. Just cut out a rectangular piece of plastic canvas, thread the lace through it while flat (see steps **1–3**), and use the last piece of lace to tie it into a cylinder (steps **4–5**). The cylinder can become a face with the hair tucked in the top (like **Musketeer**). Or you can stuff a pom-pom in the top and make the pom-pom into a head (like **Punk** or **Blue Eyes**). You can even put hair on top of a pom-pom (like **Green Gertie**).

Materials:
- 11 pieces 16-inch plastic lace
- 1 piece plastic canvas, 8 holes by 26 holes

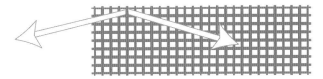

1 Starting at the left, skip the first three rows. Thread a piece of plastic lace in at the top of the fourth row and out at the top of the fifth row. Center the lengths on each side.

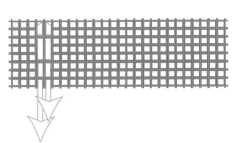

2 Going down, thread each end of the plastic lace in and out three times. Let the ends dangle free.

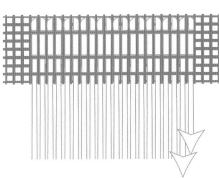

3 Repeat this nine more times. You can follow the same pattern each time, or vary it.

Blue Eyes

Musketeer

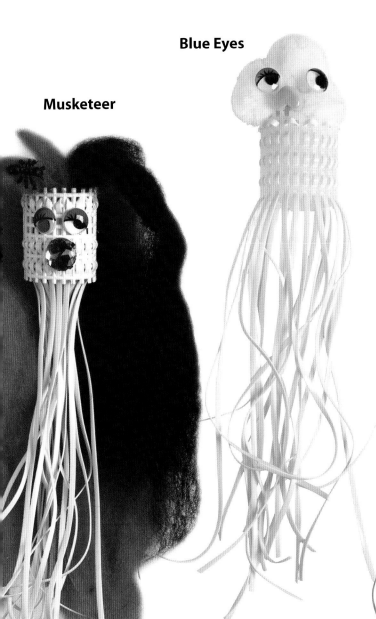

Punk

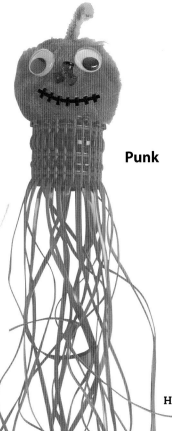

4 Now overlap the two edges of the plastic canvas by two rows, forming a cylinder. Use the last piece of plastic lace to anchor them together.

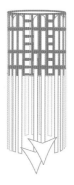

5 Lace as before. This time you are lacing through two thicknesses of plastic canvas, so hold them firmly together. It will still be the hardest lace to do, because of the narrow space inside. Make sure the lace stays flat and doesn't twist. There will be an empty row on each side of the final anchor lace.

Now you can work on the front to form one of the various faces. In creating *your* creature, you can imitate one of ours, or mix any of the components to create a brand new creature all your own!

Head and Hair

Pom-Pom Head: Apply a thin line of glue just inside top rim. Press pom-pom in gently. Use pom-pom alone, or drape acrylic hair over it as with **Wart Nose**.

Acrylic Hair: Press into top of cylinder. Create an upsweep as with **Fang** and **Mr. Brow**. Or let it drape downward as with **Musketeer**. Try mixing two colors as with **Musketeer** and **Wart Nose**.

Chenille Stem Hair: Cut short or long pieces of chenille stems to create curly strands of hair as with **Bead Head**.

Wart Nose

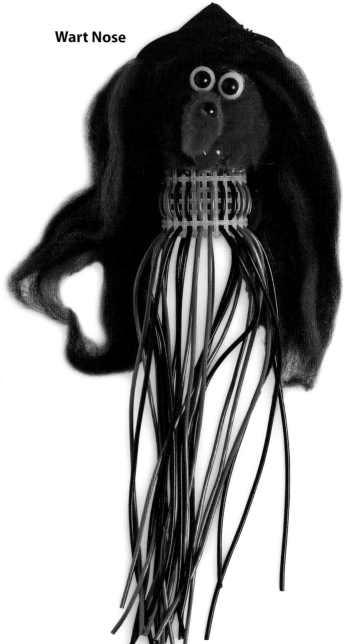

Bead Head

Mr. Brow

Eyes

Stick-on craft eyes, round or oval

Pony beads or other beads

Fashion drops (stick-on earrings)

Eyelashes

Cut fake eyelashes to fit any eye size (**Fang**)

Or use stick-on craft eyes with eyelashes

Eyebrows

Use a chenille stem cut in one long or two small pieces (**Mr. Brow, Butterfly**)

Nose

Use a protruding single or folded chenille stem (**Green Gertie**)

Beads also work well as noses (**Punk**)

Teeth

Make teeth or fangs from tiny triangles of paper or foam (**Fang**)

Spiders, Ants and Flies

Bugs make fun decorations (**Spider Eyes**). Look around for other unusual things, too, and see how they work.

Fang

Green Gertie

Spider Eyes

Mouth

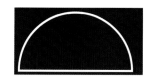

Fashion drops (stick-on earrings)

Pony beads, other beads, or stick-on gems (**Musketeer**)

Round or flat lace; remember, round lace can smile, but flat lace can't (**Spider Eyes**)

Chenille stem clippings

You can also stitch mouths and other features with plastic lace (**Bead Head**, **Stitch Lips**)

Witch's Hat

1 To make the pointed cone, take a sheet of black paper or black foam. Using a compass, make a 5-inch diameter half-circle, and cut it out.

2 Letting the center of the circle be the tip of the cone, slide the two sides over each other until the diameter of the base is 2 inches. Glue the overlap area together.

3 To make the brim, use the same piece of paper or foam. Draw a 2-inch diameter circle inside of a 3-inch diameter circle. Cut along the lines. Push the brim over the cone until it almost touches the base, and glue in place. Now you have a hat like **Green Gertie's**.

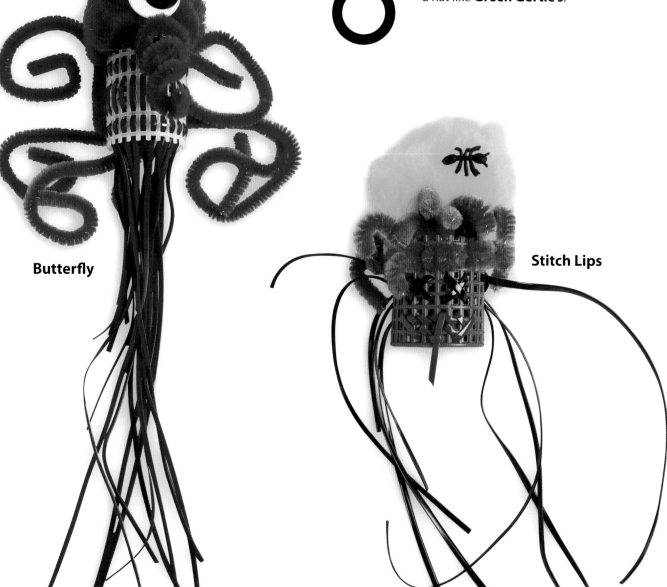

Butterfly

Stitch Lips

Maxi-Sox Creatures

Materials
- 8 pieces 36-inch orange plastic lace
- 8 pieces 36-inch black plastic lace
- 1 piece plastic canvas, 20 holes by 46 holes
- 4 pieces 6-inch chenille stem for arms
- 2 stick-on craft eyes
- Assorted beads, bugs, snakes, etc.

Make the **Maxi-Sox** similar to the **Fuzzy Creature Hangings** on the preceding pages. Leave three empty rows at each end for the final overlap stitches. Start in the center and work your way out. One pattern is shown in figure **A**. Thread a piece of orange lace in at the top of the 23rd row and out the top of the 24th row, and center it. Going down, lace each end in and out six to eight times, making a pattern of short and long stitches. Lace six to eight rows in the center where the face will be. Skipping a row, use a black lace to make two rows on each side. As you continue, make left and right symmetrical. Finally you will have three or four empty rows. Bend the rectangle of plastic into a cylinder, and use a final piece of lace to lace together the outside rows.

Enliven your Maxi-Sox creatures by adding arms (see steps **1–3**), eyelashes, eyes, and mouths. **Viper Lady** achieves a charming Medusa effect with the addition of two snakes. **Creepy Legs** uses chenille stems for legs, expressive eyebrows, and a nose.

1 To make an arm with a three-fingered hand, pick two chenille stems whose colors go nicely together. Cut them in half to 6-inch lengths. Wrap two 6-inch lengths together.

2 At 2½ inches, make a fold. Make four more folds at half-inch intervals.

3 Squeeze the base of the fingers together, and you have a hand. Make the second arm with the other two 6-inch pieces. Thread each arm through an empty hole in the side of your creature, seven or eight spaces up from the bottom. Attach each arm loosely by separating the two chenille stems inside for about a half-inch, and bending them apart.

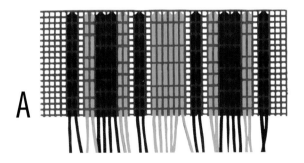

A

Creepy Legs

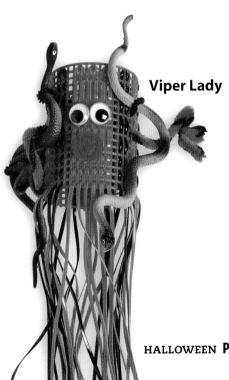

Viper Lady

Buggy Fours

Materials
- 2 pieces 42-inch plastic lace
- Assorted spiders, ants, flies, pony beads
- 1 lanyard hook

This four-strand stitch is the simplest stitch and the secret behind many a cool project. Follow the step-by-step instructions and use the photos as extra references.

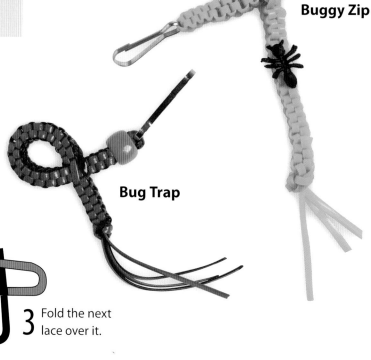

Buggy Zip

Bug Trap

1 Thread the strands of plastic lace through the lanyard hook until the hook is at the middle of the laces.

2 Fasten down with a piece of tape for the first stitch; remove the tape after step **5**. Fold one lace over.

3 Fold the next lace over it.

4 Fold the third lace over the second.

5 Fold the fourth lace over the third and under the loop formed by the first one.

6 Remove the tape, and pull the stitch tight.

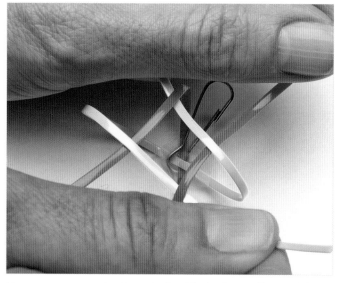

Here you can see the first stitch with the lace still taped down (step **5**).

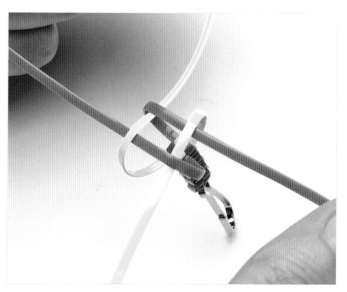

A regular stitch will look like this before you tighten it (step **10a**).

The Square Stitch

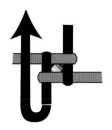

7a To make a square stitch (like **Bug Trap**), first fold the first strand over itself.

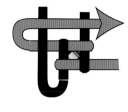

8a Fold the other laces one at a time; starting here with the second strand, fold it over itself.

9a Fold the third strand over itself.

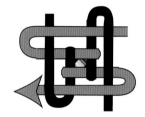

10a Fold the fourth strand over itself, making sure to thread it under the loop formed by the first strand.

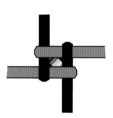

11a Tighten the stitch.

12a As you continue making square stitches, the box pattern will appear.

The Round Stitch

7b To make a round stitch (like **Buggy Zip**), fold the first strand over the opposite one, at an angle.

8b Fold the adjacent strand over it, again at an angle.

9b Fold the third strand at an angle.

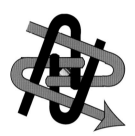

10b Fold the fourth strand at an angle, making sure to thread it through the loop of the first strand.

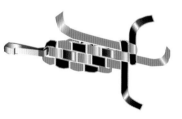

12b Tighten; this stitch is rotated from the first. Make the second and succeeding stitches the same as the first. If it went clockwise, continue clockwise; if it went counterclockwise, continue counter-clockwise. As you continue making round stitches, the spiral pattern will appear.

Making the Loop

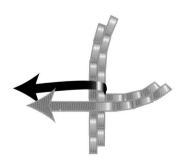

13 To make your project loop like **Buggy Zip** and **Bug Trap**, continue with your square or round stitch until you have laced 2–3 inches. Make a loop, bringing the end up against the side about a half-inch from the start. Bring two strands over the top and two under the bottom.

14 Following the same steps you used before (**2–5**), unite the strands together, and start a new stitch on the opposite side. When you've made another 25 stitches, it's time to finish the project.

See page 12 for finishing.

Finishing

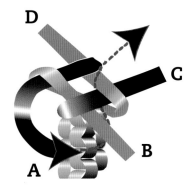

15 To finish your project, make a final square stitch, and leave it loose. Run strand A under strand B and up through the center. Run strand B under C and up the center. Continue with C and D, so all ends are together in the center. Now pull tight, and trim off the ends at 2 inches.

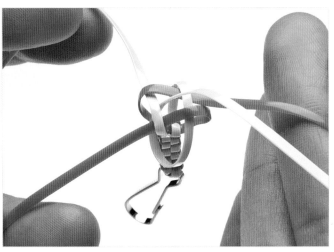

When finishing a project, you will thread each strand up through the square formed by the loose final stitch (step **15**).

Your finished four-strand project will look something like this.

Centipedes

Materials
- 2 pieces 24-inch plastic lace
- 16 pieces 2-inch plastic lace for legs (Big Centipede)
- 16 pieces 1-inch plastic lace for legs (Little Centipede)
- 1 or 2 pony beads
- 1 lanyard hook

Making the centipede is quite straightforward. You just stitch and add legs as you go along. After two initial stitches, run all four strands through one pony bead (**Little Centipede**), or run two strands through each of two pony beads (**Big Centipede**). Reunite into a square stitch. While the next stitch is still loose, run the first short leg strip through it, center, and tighten. After every second stitch, thread in a new leg strip. After the last leg, make one more stitch and finish as shown above.

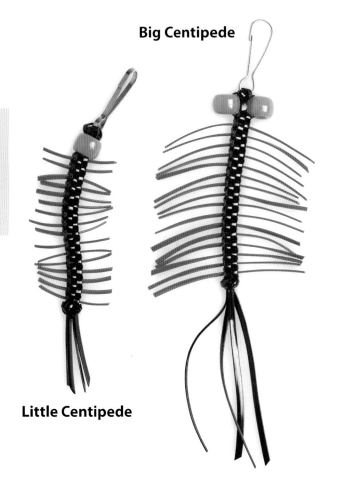

Big Centipede

Little Centipede

Bat Cat & Meow Pal

Materials
- 2 pieces 10-foot black plastic lace
- 1 black chenille stem
- 1 black or other color chenille stem
- 2 oval fashion drops or pony beads
- 1 rubber bat
- 1 lanyard hook

These charming cats use one big double loop. Follow the step-by-step instructions to make the body, then add features and decorate as described below.

Meow Pal

Bat Cat

1 Run the plastic lace through the lanyard hook temporarily, and start a square stitch as with the **Buggy Fours** on page 10. Continue with the square stitch for 10 inches. To form the body loop, bring the working end around and cross over near the start, as in steps **13** and **14** on page 11.

2 Make another 6 inches of square stitch, and close the head loop: remove the lanyard hook, and an X is visible. Thread two strands through the X from one side.

3 Then thread two strands through from the other. Cut the tips at an angle to help thread them through. Pull tight, and cut off the excess.

To form the eyes, cut one oval from the colored or black chenille stem, fold it in half, and glue the two ends to the back of the cat's head on one side. Repeat on the other side. Glue a fashion drop, pony bead, or stick-on craft eye to each chenille oval. Ears are two 2-inch lengths of black chenille stem bent at an angle and glued to the back of the head, or twisted on if you have slightly longer pieces. Whiskers are four to six 2-inch lengths of chenille stem or plastic lace twisted or glued to the front of the head. For the tail, cut a long piece of black chenille stem. Wrap one end tightly at the bottom of the body loop, and give it a little twist. Decorate the cat at the neck by gluing on a rubber bat, a bow, or a collar made of chenille stem.

Weird Six-Strand Zips

All of the little monsters described here start off as six-strand zipper pulls. **Teeny Legs** continues happily for 2 inches. Then it splits into two teeny legs. **Pretzel Ears** splits into two loops that rejoin to form the body. Then it splits into two legs. **Glow Ghost** has a neck and two arms as well as two legs.

Teeny Legs

Materials
- 1 piece 38-inch plastic lace
- 2 pieces 32-inch plastic lace
- 1 lanyard hook
- 2 stick-on craft eyes

Teeny Legs

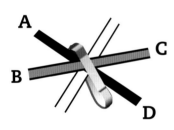

1 Thread the three pieces of plastic lace through the hook until it is at the center of each of them. Cross the two short pieces. Fasten in place with pieces of tape for the first stitch. Remove the tape after step **5**.

2 Take the longest piece and fold it over to form the two guidelines. Keep them parallel.

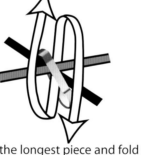

3 Place strand A (black) over the near guideline and under the loop of the far guideline.

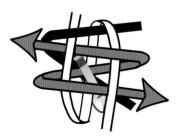

4 Similarly, place B and C (orange) over the near guideline and under the far guideline.

5 Finally run D (black) over the near guideline and under the loop of the far guideline.

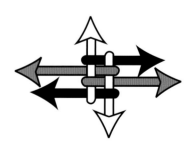

6 The stitch is complete. Remove the tape, and pull in the directions of the arrows.

The Straight Stitch

7 To make a straight stitch, first fold the two guideline laces straight back over themselves.

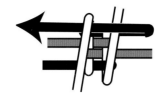

8 Following the arrows, place each lace in succession over the near guideline and under the far one, starting with the top lace (black).

9 Place the middle (orange) strands over the near guidelines and under the far guidelines.

10 Place the bottom (black) strand over the near guideline and under the loop of the far guideline.

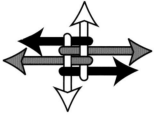

11 Tighten the stitch. If you are making **Teeny Legs**, continue the straight stitch for 2 inches.

Making the Legs

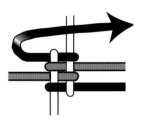

12 To form the legs, split the six strands into two groups of three. Run one strand back over itself.

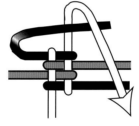

13 Run the next strand over it.

14 Run the third strand over the second and under the loop of the first.

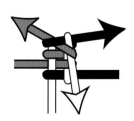

15 Pull tight, and see the triangular form take shape.

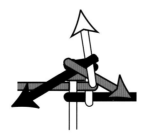

16 Continue, folding each strand over itself. Lace only four stitches this way. Make the same number of stitches on the other leg.

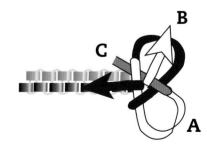

17 To finish off, run strand A under B and up the center. Run B under C and up the center. Finally run C underneath and up the center, and tighten.

Pretzel Ears

Materials
- 1 piece 52-inch plastic lace
- 2 pieces 42-inch plastic lace
- 1 lanyard hook
- 2 stick-on craft eyes

With its huge ears, your little monster can warn you of approaching dangers. Glue on a couple of eyes or antennae, and he'll really be a sentinel for you. This project uses six strands and incorporates some twists and turns.

Pretzel Ears

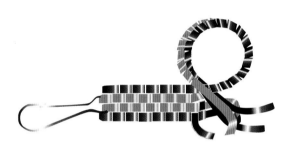

1 Start a six-strand zipper pull. Continue it for ten stitches. Open into two columns of three strands each (steps **12–16**, page 15). Lace one column for 20 stitches. Cross it over itself close to the beginning as shown. Make four more stitches. Do the same with the second column. Now you have two big ears floating free.

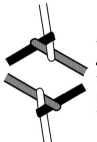

2 To reunite them, have the two long strands pointing away from each other.

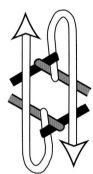

3 Fold them back to form the guidelines, and hold them in place with one hand.

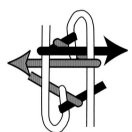

4 Fold one outside lace over the near guideline and under the loop of the far guideline. Do the same for the first inside lace.

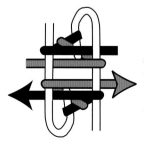

5 Fold the second inside lace and the second outside lace over and under the guidelines.

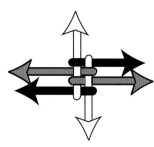

6 Pull all ends tight as they were in the original six-strand zipper pull. Make 12 more stitches. Open into two three-strand columns for the legs. Make ten stitches on each leg, and finish as in step **17** on page 15.

Glow Ghosts

Materials
- 1 piece 32-inch plastic lace
- 2 pieces 26-inch plastic lace
- 3 pieces 10-inch plastic lace
- 1 lanyard hook
- 2 stick-on craft eyes

Glow Ghost

Try making these ghosts with glow-in-the-dark plastic lace for a cool effect.

 **1** Start a six-strand project as on page 14, and make 7 stitches. To form the neck, let the two central strands dangle free. Use the other four strands to make a square stitch around them.

 2 Make three square stitches. Now spread the two central strands out.

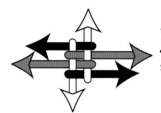 **3** Weave them into a six-strand straight stitch.

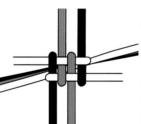 **4** Make two tight stitches and one loose one. Group the three short lace pieces together. Thread them under the loose stitch, parallel to and between the two guideline laces. Make sure both sides are equal in length. Pull the stitch tight. Make ten more straight stitches with your main body lace.

To form the legs, split the six strands into two groups of three as on page 15, steps **12–16**. Make ten triangular stitches on each leg, and finish (page 15, step **17**). Lace the arms in the same triangular stitch from the shoulders out. After six stitches, finish off as you did the legs. Trim the loose ends to about a half-inch. Fasten the eyes with a small dab of glue.

Beady Eyes

Additional Materials
- 2 pony beads
- 2 black half-rounds (optional)

Beady Eyes

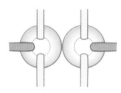 **5** **Beady Eyes** is a variation of Glow Ghosts. After starting and making two stitches, run three strands through one pony bead and three through the other.

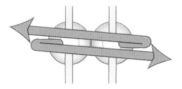 **6** Reunite into a six-strand column: first fold the guidelines as shown.

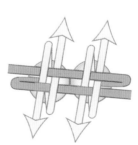 **7** Then continue with six-strand stitches as above. The last step is to glue optional half-rounds onto the beads or use marker to give the eyes more detail.

Snake Key Chain

Materials
- 2 pieces 36-inch plastic lace
- 1 piece 48-inch plastic lace
- 1 plastic or rubber snake
- 1 key ring

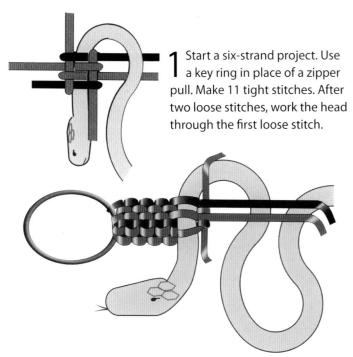

1 Start a six-strand project. Use a key ring in place of a zipper pull. Make 11 tight stitches. After two loose stitches, work the head through the first loose stitch.

2 Tighten the two stitches to hold the head firmly. Make five more tight stitches. Lace a stitch over the second curve of the snake. Fasten the second curve with tight stitches. Do ten stitches. Lace a stitch over the third curve of the snake, and continue. After another seven stitches, enclose the fourth curve near the tail. Continue for another nine stitches. After 3½ to 4 inches, finish off.

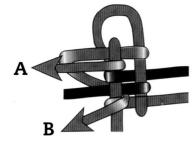

3 To finish a six-strand project, make a final straight stitch, and leave it loose. Run lace A around the next lace, under and up the center. Run lace B around the next lace, under and up the center. Do the same with the others until all six laces are in the center. Tighten, and trim.

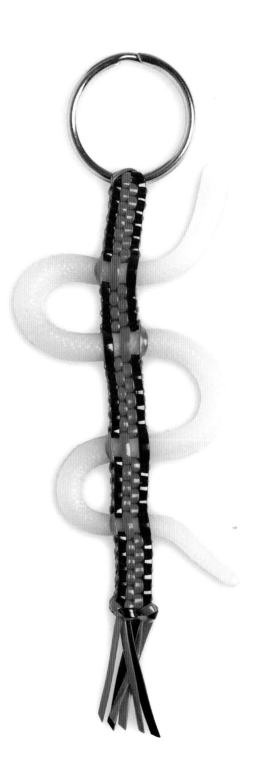